THE JOY

OF LESS

JOURNAL

Clear Your Inner Clutter

FRANCINE JAY

CHRONICLE BOOKS
SAN FRANCISCO

Introduction

When we declutter our homes, something wonderful happens: for each item we release, we regain a little bit of space. As we continue to let go, that space spreads out–creating a sense of openness and airiness, and restoring peace and potential to our abodes.

But here's something even more extraordinary: the space doesn't need to stop there. We can take our minimalist practice a step further and let that glorious space into our minds, hearts, and souls. Just as we clear away the physical junk, we can clear away the psychological and emotional junk, giving our very beings a new lightness and serenity.

In *The Joy of Less* (the companion book to this journal), we learned the STREAMLINE method–ten surefire steps to purge our excess possessions. By applying these techniques, and changing our perspective on stuff, we freed ourselves from the physical clutter weighing us down.

But can we really declutter our worries and stresses the way we decluttered our socks? We sure can! We just have to be good gatekeepers of our inner lives and realize that we don't have to hold on to every feeling, commitment, or expectation that comes our way. We must question them as deliberately and thoroughly as we did the items in our homes–asking whether they enhance our lives or detract from them.

Granted, it's a little trickier to examine a feeling than it is a piece of furniture—but that's what this journal is for. Writing helps us dump out the mental clutter, shine the light of day on it, and determine once and for all what to keep or toss. We'll give our thoughts and emotions the same inquisition that we gave our stuff—What are you? How did you get here? Are you worth having in my life?—and decide whether we're better off letting them go.

Over the course of this journal, we'll ponder various ways to Reduce Stress. Commitments, expectations, and responsibilities pile up over the months and years, and rarely do we take the time (we don't have any!) to purge them. The result: lots of less meaningful activities crowd out the more meaningful ones, leaving us weary and unfulfilled. Worse yet, our busyness can take a toll on our mental health, making us feel frustrated, helpless, and overwhelmed by our daily lives. As we write, we'll strive to identify and eliminate our excess stressors and the pressures that go along with them. In so doing, we'll regain a sense of empowerment and control over our lives, making for more-rewarding days and more-restful nights.

We'll also write to Release Worries. (You may be surprised how powerful and life-changing this can be!) When we squirrel away negative feelings the way we do our stuff, they weigh on us and steal our joy. But now their days are numbered: one by one, we're going to shake them out, see them for what they are, and send them on their way. When we do a clean sweep of our hearts, that old grudge, nagging guilt, or buried anger will no longer have a place to hide. Writing helps us identify our emotions in a detached, objective way–Hello, anxiety. What are you doing here?–and say good-bye to those that aren't serving us well.

As we clear out the mental clutter, we Restore Clarity. This is the ultimate goal of our minimalist journey: to eliminate the extraneous, so as to focus on what's truly special to us. We'll explore various techniques to calm our muddy waters, filter out the detritus, and see what emerges from the clear and sparkling depths. We'll contemplate what nourishes our souls and gives us a higher sense of purpose–whether it's pursuing a passion, contributing to our community, or spending more time with our kids–and commit our time, attention, and resources to that end. The point of emptying our cups is that they stand ready to be filled with our hopes, dreams, and joy.

It's time to clear the way to a lighter, more serene life. The fifty-two prompts that follow–which you can work through weekly or at your own pace–will inspire and support you on your journey. Letting go may be challenging at first, but with practice can become as natural and delightful as a child blowing a dandelion. So pick up your pen, take a deep breath, and release your (inner) clutter to the wind. . . .

KEY

O   *Reduce Stress*

↯   *Release Worries*

✳   *Restore Clarity*

"In space cometh grace."

–*John Heywood*

○ LET GO OF AN EXPECTATION

Expectations sound great in theory—Who doesn't want to be
the perfect parent, spouse, employee, or friend?—but in reality,
they cause all kinds of stress. The problem: they're often set so
high that they're nearly unattainable.

Write down one expectation that stresses you out—it can be one
you've set for yourself, someone else, or a certain situation. Is it
unrealistic, and if so, why? What (if anything) would happen if
this expectation wasn't met? How would it feel to release it?

'Hack your Anxiety' Alicia H. Clark
pg. 20
"I have grown to see that anxiety is really a
sign that something we care about is at risk
and we might not be able to protect it."
"However it manifests itself anxiety is grounded
in a cause"

Self

"Blessed is he who expects nothing, for he shall never be disappointed."

—ALEXANDER POPE

✳ SINGLE-TASK

When we multitask, we're never fully focused on one thing–leaving us distracted, confused, and less than precise in our work. Single-tasking, on the other hand, allows us to act with concentration and clarity. When we devote our full attention to one activity at a time, it makes for a more pleasurable process and better results.

Write down an activity you will single-task today. It could be working on a project (without checking email), playing with your toddler (without chatting on your phone), or cooking a meal (without turning on the TV). Return to this page later and record how it made you feel. Did you find the activity easier? More enjoyable? More rewarding?

"To do two things
at once is to do
neither."

–Publilius Syrus

⚘ LET GO OF A WORRY

We all have worries—over our jobs, our kids, our health, our relationships, and so on. But when we dwell on our troubles (real or imagined), we drain the energies we could be using for more uplifting thoughts and pursuits. Worries neither bring us joy nor accomplish anything, so the more of them we can declutter, the better!

What particular worry would you like to release? Rather than ruminating over it, could you take more positive action to address it? How would you feel if you simply let it go? (Lighter? Happier? More serene?)

"We suffer more often in imagination than in reality."

—SENECA

✳ SLOW DOWN

Busy has become standard in our society, compelling us to speed through our days to "get it all done." But when we're moving so fast, we miss the important things in life. Our families, our friends, our passions, hopes, and dreams become a blur as we rush by.

Think of one way you can slow down today. Can you relax with a cup of coffee instead of drinking it on the go? Take a leisurely walk with your partner or child? Have a long talk with a friend instead of texting? What to-do can you eliminate to make the time?

"There is more
to life than increasing
its speed."

–*Gandhi*

◯ LET GO OF A COMMITMENT

We can't do everything, please everyone, and be everywhere at the same time—but that won't stop others from asking us to do so. But remember, just as every object takes away space in our homes, every task takes away space in our schedules—and saying no to a less important activity means saying yes to a more important one.

Think of a commitment that leaves you less than fulfilled. Is it essential? How can you eliminate it from your schedule? What can you do with the time and energy freed up by its absence?

"The chains which cramp us most are those which weigh on us least."

—MADAME SWETCHINE

✳ FOCUS ON A COMMITMENT

When we have too many commitments, we're often forced to give them half-hearted efforts. And even though we've met them on the surface, we feel a little uneasy that we didn't give our best.

Choose one commitment to which you'll give a full and genuine effort. (Perhaps you'll embrace your responsibilities as a PTA member or be truly present and engaged when paying a visit to an elderly relative.) How will giving it your all bring more joy and satisfaction to the activity?

"Whatever is worth
doing at all is worth
doing well."

–Philip Stanhope, 4th Earl of Chesterfield

✎ LET GO OF A REGRET

Regrets are rooted in the past. We may wish we had done things differently, but unless we can go back in time, we have little power to change them. What we *can* do, however, is focus on our present actions and align them with our values and goals. We can then make peace with our past and move on.

Write down a regret you'd like to purge from your heart. What steps can you take to let it go? Perhaps you can apologize or make amends for a wrongdoing, or attempt to course-correct a wrong turn. Or, upon reflection, you may realize that although you regret something (not getting a certain degree or making a relationship work), life still turned out okay and the lessons learned helped you grow.

_____

_____

_____

_____

_____

_____

_____

_____

_____

_____

_____

_____

_____

_____

_____

"What cannot be repaired is not to be regretted."

–SAMUEL JOHNSON

✳ SAVOR

All too often, we go through life on autopilot, forgetting to enjoy the magic and enchantment of our time here on earth. That's why we want to simplify our lives—so we can live mindfully in the present and savor every precious moment.

In fact, let's start right now. Savor *this* moment—write down what you see, what you hear, what you smell, what you feel, what you think ("I see the sun shining through the window. I hear children playing outside. I smell coffee brewing . . ."). Bring this practice into your daily life—whether you're taking a walk or just taking out the trash—and let yourself be dazzled by the splendor of this world.

"Live in the sunshine,
swim the sea,
Drink the wild air's
salubrity."

–Ralph Waldo Emerson

○ LET GO OF A TIMESINK

Sometimes we have no idea where our time goes—but over the course of our day, we've frittered away fifteen minutes here, thirty minutes there, checking email, reading blogs, or engaging in other fun-but-frivolous timesinks.

What unproductive activity or distraction can you purge from your day? If you don't want to eliminate it entirely, can you set a time limit for it or schedule it for a part of the day (such as over lunch or before bed) when it won't distract you from more meaningful tasks?

"Dost thou love life? Then waste not time,
for time is the stuff that life is made of."

–BENJAMIN FRANKLIN

✳ BE SILENT

The world can be a noisy place, and it's often hard to think clearly amid the din of televisions, radios, phones, computers, and even our own voices. Silence, on the other hand, can be a wellspring of clarity—helping us tune in to ourselves and discover who we really are.

How can you reduce the background noise in your daily life? (Turn off the television? Take off the headphones? Mute your phone for a few hours each day?) When your world is quieter, listen carefully to the sounds around you. What do you hear? Listen for your inner voice. What is it telling you?

"Let us be silent,–so
we may hear the whisper
of the gods."

–*Ralph Waldo Emerson*

_____

_____

_____

_____

_____

_____

_____

_____

_____

_____

_____

_____

_____

_____

_____

_____

_____

*"True silence is the rest of the mind, and is to the spirit what
sleep is to the body, nourishment and refreshment."*

—WILLIAM PENN

LET GO OF A GRUDGE

When we hold a grudge, we cling to feelings of hurt, resentment, and hostility—feelings that can crowd out or prevent us from experiencing more joyous aspects of life. It stays an open wound, causing us pain long after the original injustice occurred.

Think of a grudge you're holding. How does it make you feel? Now imagine releasing that grudge and all the negative emotions surrounding it. Do you feel a weight lifted from your shoulders? What steps can you take to forgive, forget, and move forward?

_____

_____

_____

_____

_____

_____

_____

_____

_____

_____

_____

_____

_____

_____

"To err is human; to forgive, divine."

—ALEXANDER POPE

The more we simplify our lives, the greater serenity we achieve. We only have so many hours each day, and the fewer we devote to the frivolous, the more we can devote to what matters.

Write down three aspects of your day you can simplify. Some examples: your beauty routine, your online activity, your daily workout. For each one, list specific steps you can take to streamline it (like skipping the mud mask or closing a social media account).

"Our life is
frittered away by detail. . . .
Simplify, simplify."

–Henry David Thoreau

○ LET GO OF A PROJECT OR HOBBY

Don't feel obligated to finish every project you've initiated or pursue every hobby you've dabbled in. When we engage in too many pastimes (even if we enjoy them), we never have the opportunity to explore or master anything in depth—leaving us with little sense of satisfaction or accomplishment.

Describe an unfinished project or outgrown hobby you'd like to abandon and why. If you're not driven by a burning desire to complete it—whether it's that half-knit sweater, half-built book-shelf, or half-written novel—give yourself permission to give it up and move on.

_____

_____

_____

_____

_____

_____

_____

_____

_____

_____

_____

_____

_____

"Let your affairs be as two or three, and not a hundred or a thousand."

–HENRY DAVID THOREAU

"He who begins many things finishes but few."

−PROVERB

✳ BE STILL

It's difficult to practice mindfulness when we're always in motion—running here, running there, doing this and that. For a few minutes each day, just sit still and be. Bring stillness to your thoughts as well as your body. Only when you calm the waters of your mind can you see into its depths.

For five minutes, be completely still—really, truly not-moving-a-muscle still. Don't cling to any thoughts; if they bubble to the surface, let them go. Afterward, write down how this exercise made you feel. Were you surprised by any thoughts that arose? What are other opportunities to practice stillness each day? (On the bus? At your desk? In line at the bank?)

"Muddy water,
let stand,
becomes clear."

–Lao Tzu

⚘ LET GO OF A GUILT

We all make mistakes, and sometimes feel like we've wronged someone or let them down. We may even feel bad about the smallest of slights or about circumstances beyond our control. But instead of letting guilty feelings weigh on us, we need to channel our energies into making things right.

Write down one thing you feel guilty about. Is your guilt justified? Is the situation serious enough to warrant your mental and emotional energy? If so, consider how you can make amends. Do you need to ask for forgiveness? Do you need to forgive yourself? What other steps can you take to restore your peace of mind?

_____

_____

_____

_____

_____

_____

_____

_____

_____

_____

_____

_____

_____

"There is no pillow so soft as a clear conscience."

–FRENCH PROVERB

✳ CULTIVATE SOPHROSYNE

Sophrosyne is a classical Greek ideal of achieving happiness through mindful living. It involves self-knowledge (knowing what's enough), self-restraint (choosing enough over excess), and harmony (finding joy in enough). Sophrosyne isn't about choosing less for its own sake, but rather the happiness it brings us. It's living a wise, graceful, and balanced life because we wouldn't have it any other way.

Sophrosyne isn't skipping dessert and feeling miserable about it; it's eating healthy foods, in healthy proportions, because it makes your body feel better. Sophrosyne isn't denying yourself that trendy "must-have" item and feeling deprived; it's being excited to preserve the earth's resources. Sophrosyne isn't about choosing moderation because you think you *should*, but because it feels right and delights your soul.

List three ways in which you can practice sophrosyne (such as scaling back your spending or screen time). How will embracing "enough" in these activities enhance your life?

"Out of moderation
a pure happiness springs."

–Johann Wolfgang von Goethe

○ LET GO OF A DRAMA

Let's admit it, there's a little bit of drama queen (or king) in all of us. Sometimes we just can't help overreacting, making a mountain out of a molehill, or meddling in someone else's business. Unfortunately, this excess drama can take a real toll on our psychological well-being.

What particular drama can you eliminate from your life? A family feud? A conflict with a coworker? An oversensitivity to others' remarks? What steps can you take to let go of this drama, and how will you feel when it's gone? (Relieved? Peaceful? Free?)

_"We might have much peace if we would not busy ourselves
with the sayings and doings of others."_

–THOMAS À KEMPIS

✳ BE SATISFIED

We always seem to have our sights set on more (money, possessions, accolades), better (car, clothes, job title), and bigger (house, television, paycheck) and run ourselves ragged to achieve it. Minimalism helps us recognize we already have *enough*, so we can relax and enjoy it.

Write down one better thing you want, one bigger thing you want, and something you want more of. Is it worth the sacrifices you're making (long hours, high stress, money) to acquire them? Can you just as well get by, and be happy, with what you already have?

"Contentment consists
not in great wealth,
but in few wants."

–Epictetus

"With a few flowers in my garden, half a dozen pictures,
and some books, I live without envy."

–LOPE DE VEGA

⚘ LET GO OF A SADNESS

When we experience tragedies and difficult situations, it's natural and healthy to feel sadness. But there comes a time when the sorrow has served its purpose and clinging to it only prolongs the pain.

Are you carrying a sadness you'd like to release? Write down what you've learned from the experience. What ray of sunshine can part these clouds of sorrow?

"One joy scatters a hundred griefs."

–CHINESE PROVERB

✳ PRACTICE SELF-CARE

We're often so busy tending to the needs of others that we forget, or neglect, to take care of our own. But in order to function at our best, we must maintain our own physical and mental well-being. A little self-care keeps you balanced and centered and can simplify your life by helping you avoid health problems.

List three things you can do to nurture yourself. It may be taking time to have a healthy meal, going for a walk, meditating, or simply soaking in the tub. How can you carve out some time in your schedule to care for yourself?

"Take rest;
a field that has rested
gives a bountiful crop."

–Ovid

○ LET GO OF A GOAL

Goals can be wonderful motivators–but if we don't allow them to change and evolve, they can cause stress, exhaustion, and burnout. Instead of rigidly adhering to your goals, see them as wildflowers, growing and fading with the seasons. Goals you set last year may no longer be as relevant now; instead of forcing them to bloom, let them go to seed, so you can embrace new ones that arise in their place.

Which of your goals no longer stirs your soul? Is it a source of stress or frustration rather than joy or self-discovery? Does it take away energy and resources better spent on something more inspiring? How would it feel to weed it out?

_____

_____

_____

_____

_____

_____

_____

_____

_____

_____

_____

_____

_____

_____

_____

_____

_____

"Change in all things is sweet."

–ARISTOTLE

✳ FOCUS ON A GOAL

Too many goals often means too little progress. We need to identify the important ones, so we can pursue them without distraction. When we channel our resources and energy into a chosen few, we're much more likely to achieve them.

Write down one goal on which you'll concentrate your efforts. Can you break it down into a series of smaller, actionable steps? What milestones can you set to track your progress?

"To follow,
without halt, one aim:
There's the secret
of success."

–*Anna Pavlova*

✲ LET GO OF A DISAPPOINTMENT

Life is full of disappointments—it's how we handle them that makes all the difference. Don't keep them as souvenirs of what didn't go your way; brooding over them won't change anything. Toss them out and focus your thoughts on more positive outcomes.

Write down one disappointment you'd like to declutter. Why didn't things work out the way you'd hoped? Can you find a silver lining in this letdown?

_____

_____

_____

_____

_____

_____

_____

_____

_____

_____

_____

_____

_____

_____

_____

_____

*"If we will be quiet and ready enough, we shall find
compensation in every disappointment."*

–HENRY DAVID THOREAU

✳ FIND YOUR FORTE

We all have a special gift, talent, or thing at which we excel—be it dancing, cooking, writing, listening, painting, programming, or parenting. When we clear the excess from our lives, we gain the time and clarity to discover our forte.

Use these pages to explore your forte. What do you love to do? What have you always been told you're "good at"? What activity makes your heart sing and your soul come alive? Once you've found your forte, what can you do to develop it further?

"Whatever you are,
be a good one."

–William Makepeace Thackeray

○ LET GO OF A CONSTRAINT

What do you feel is holding you back from accomplishing one of your goals? What feels constraining in your life?

Write it down here and brainstorm some ways to overcome it. If it's a lack of time, ponder how you can rearrange your schedule to free an hour a day. If it's a lack of space, think how you can carve out a dedicated nook in your home. If it's a lack of confidence, write down the talents and skills you possess to be successful—or how you can go about acquiring them.

_____

_____

_____

_____

_____

_____

_____

_____

_____

_____

_____

_____

_____

_____

_____

"The greater the obstacle, the more glory in overcoming it."

—MOLIÈRE

✳ LEARN FROM A FAILURE

We all experience our share of failures—but the part they play in our lives is in the perception. If we see failures as lessons rather than liabilities, they can be important stepping stones to our success. When we let go of our feelings surrounding failure, we can more willingly let it guide us in the right direction.

Write down one of your failures. What's the most important thing you learned from the experience and how will you use that knowledge moving forward?

"Every failure
is a step to success."

–*William Whewell*

🌿 LET GO OF A DESIRE

Buddha taught that desires lie at the root of all suffering, for our inability to fulfill them causes unhappiness. Even fulfilled desires often lead to new ones, leaving us perpetually unsatisfied. We're consumed by want of something and can't rest until it's ours—then when it is, we start a new cycle of wanting. Conversely, when we eliminate our desires, we find peace.

What desire can you declutter? (It can be as simple as a new outfit or as lofty as fame and fortune.) Will your life go on just as well without it? How do you feel about letting it go? (Relaxed? Relieved? Indifferent?)

"How many things are there which I do not want."

–SOCRATES

✳ BE A BUTTERFLY

A butterfly flits gracefully through life with the barest of essentials. It doesn't pine for the past or fret about the future, but lives entirely in the present moment. It exists harmoniously with nature and inspires others with its beauty.

List a few ways you can live as lightly, gracefully, and beautifully as a butterfly. How can you live in the moment? How can you lighten your load? How can you speak and act with more poise, elegance, and kindness?

"Grace is the outcome
of inward harmony."

–Marie Ebner-Eschenbach

We invest a lot in our relationships–and therefore tend to cling to them, even when they're not working out. Some can be simply unrewarding, while others can be downright toxic. Bottom line: if they're not mutually beneficial, they're taking precious time and energy from both parties' lives.

On this page, write a Dear John letter to that acquaintance, friend, or lover with whom you'd like to part ways. You don't have to send it, of course–but simply putting your feelings on paper can help *you* make the break.

"It is better to be alone than in bad company."

−PROVERB

✳ FOCUS ON A RELATIONSHIP

Our hours are precious and best devoted to the people most dear to us. When we let go of unfulfilling relationships, we have more time and energy to cultivate those we cherish.

Write down one relationship on which you'd like to focus. How does this relationship enrich your life? What do you love about this person? What are some ways you can devote more attention to them and deepen your bond?

"The only way
to have a friend is
to be one."

–Ralph Waldo Emerson

✂ LET GO OF AN ANGER

Anger is a natural response to an injustice, be it regarding a person, situation, or social issue. Holding on to it, however, takes a negative toll on our minds and bodies. It not only clouds our thoughts and makes us miserable, but can cause headaches, heart problems, high blood pressure, and digestive issues as well.

Is there something that makes your blood boil? Write down exactly why you're so mad. Are there action steps you can take to resolve the situation? If not, can you channel your anger into something positive instead, such as writing a poem or volunteering for a cause?

"Man should forget his anger before he lies down to sleep."

–THOMAS DE QUINCEY

✳ ACCEPT MUJO

Mujo, a central tenet of Zen Buddhism, means impermanence–everything is changing in every moment, and nothing stays the same. Why is this important in our minimalist journey? Because when we see that nothing is permanent, we stop clinging to people and possessions, past and present situations. When we accept mujo, we're able to let go.

Write down three ways you can accept mujo in your life (such as deciding to age gracefully instead of clinging to youth, acccpting your kids' growing independence instead of clinging to their child-hood, or being open to new ideas instead of clinging to old ones). How does it feel to give up control, go with the flow, and let things evolve of their own accord?

"Seek not that
the things which happen
should happen as you wish;
but wish the things which
happen to be as they are,
and you will have a
tranquil flow of life."

–Epictetus

⭘ LET GO OF A BAD HABIT

Bad habits are a particularly tenacious form of clutter. We can't really box them up and put them on the curb, and even after we've kicked them out, they sometimes reappear.

That's where this journal comes in handy. Make a written commitment to purge one bad habit—such as smoking, biting your nails, or watching too much TV. Can you replace it with an alternate activity or form of stress relief, like calling a friend or going for a run? Come back to this page daily or weekly to remind yourself of your goal and record your progress. Be gentle with yourself—it often takes more than one try to break a habit.

_____

_____

_____

_____

_____

_____

_____

_____

_____

_____

_____

_____

_____

_____

"Habit is either the best of servants or the worst of masters."

–NATHANIEL EMMONS

✳ FOCUS ON A GOOD HABIT

Establishing one good habit can transform your life. How? Good habits have a feel-good factor that creates a ripple effect—improving one area of your life often leads to others. For example: you decide to take a daily walk or run, which inspires you to eat healthier, which helps reduce your stress, which makes you more patient, and so on.

Write down one good habit you'd like to develop and the steps you'll take to implement it in your life. Record your progress and check back on it weekly.

"Habits form character
and character is destiny."

–Joseph Kaines

✦ LET GO OF A JUDGMENT

When we habitually judge things (or people), we put an undue burden on our mind and unnecessary restrictions on our happiness. Imagine you're at a dinner party and you're served a food and seated next to a person you "don't like"–you may very well be miserable. But if you see them as a food and a person with good qualities waiting to be discovered, you'll have a much more pleasant evening. The same goes for life.

Write down something you "don't like." Then replace your negative opinion with a positive one (such as "Brussels sprouts are nutritious" or "my boss organizes a charity drive each year"). Seeing the good in everything is a wonderful step toward a serene and happy life.

"There is nothing either good or bad, but thinking makes it so."

✳ LIVE A HAIKU LIFE

Haiku are ultra-compact Japanese poems of just seventeen syllables. They're wonderful examples of elegance and economy, full of meaning and containing nothing superfluous. Every word is precious and chosen with the utmost care.

How can you live a haiku life—in other words, bring the same mindfulness and "less is more" philosophy to the words you speak, the activities in which you participate, and the possessions you own? In what aspects of your life can you choose quality over quantity?

"Beauty of style
and harmony and grace
and good rhythm
depend on simplicity."

–Plato

"In character, in manner, in style, in all things,
the supreme excellence is simplicity."

–HENRY WADSWORTH LONGFELLOW

○ LET GO OF A TO-DO

Our to-do lists can become as overstuffed as our drawers and closets—every now and then, we have to declutter them. Upon examination, you'll likely find tasks that require too much effort for too little reward. Instead of struggling to do them, take joy in leaving them undone.

What item on your to-do list could you leave undone? Would the world stop spinning if you didn't complete it? How will you enjoy the newfound time? (Read a novel? Take a nap? Play with your child?)

"Most of those things, which we either speak or do, are unnecessary."

–MARCUS AURELIUS

✳ FOCUS ON A TO-DO

When we have a lot of to-dos, we often end up with a lot of half-dones. Instead of jumping between tasks, complete each one in turn—focus on it, finish it, and knock it off the list.

What to-do can you focus on? What distractions will you tune out in order to complete it? How will this task feel when it has your full attention? What's the most effective and expedient way to tackle it?

"Concentrate
all your thoughts
upon the work at hand.
The sun's rays do
not burn until brought
to a focus."

–*Alexander Graham Bell*

✭ LET GO OF A FEAR

Fears—be they of the dark, the dentist, heights, germs, flying, or failure—take away our freedom and keep us from fully experiencing life. They may require some work to declutter (facing them, analyzing them, and taking action against them), but the effort is well worth it. When we break free from their shackles, we can live up to our fullest potential.

Write down one of the fears you'd like to conquer. What steps can you take to let it go? (For example: If you're afraid of flying, you can read a book or take a course on conquering the phobia. If you're afraid of public speaking, you can join Toastmasters or a similar group.) When this fear is gone, what opportunities will be open to you?

"Always do what you are afraid to do."

–RALPH WALDO EMERSON

✳ EMBRACE LAGOM

The Swedes have a lovely little word for "just the right amount"– *lagom*. Lagom is that perfect balance between too much and too little, that sweet spot of having just enough.

List ways you can achieve lagom in your life. For example: a small shelf of your favorite books is more lagom than an overflowing or empty one; a schedule with a handful of fulfilling activities is more lagom than doing it all or doing nothing.

"Simplicity
is making the journey
of this life with just
baggage enough."

–Charles Dudley Warner

○ LET GO OF AN OVERINDULGENCE

When we overeat, overdrink, overshop, or otherwise overindulge, we bring excess into our lives—be it excess pounds, possessions, or other problems. When we practice moderation, on the other hand, we can enjoy such activities while maintaining our long-term well-being.

Write down one thing in which you tend to overindulge. How can you enjoy it in moderation? (Examples: skip the seconds, stop at one glass of wine, say no to impulse purchases.)

"It is best to rise from life as from a banquet, neither thirsty nor drunken."

—ARISTOTLE

✳ DO A CLEAN SWEEP

In Japan, *osouji* is an annual, ritualistic cleaning of homes and workplaces in preparation for the New Year. It's both a physical and symbolic clean sweep of clutter, purifying the space and allowing for a fresh start.

Write down the corners of your life that could use a clean sweep (like your closets, your inbox, your schedule, your worries) and how you'll eliminate the dust and debris.

"Character
must be kept bright,
as well as clean."

–Philip Stanhope, 4th Earl of Chesterfield

🌿 LET GO OF A JEALOUSY

Happiness lies in wanting what you have—not what someone else does. The best way to rid yourself of envy is to recognize and appreciate the abundance in your own life.

Write down a jealousy you'd like to jettison. How does it make you feel? Now turn things around and write down three things you're grateful for. (For example: Sometimes I feel jealous of my sister's big new house. But I'm grateful for my own house, my lovely neighborhood, and my wonderful family.) See how blessed you already are?

_____

_____

_____

_____

_____

_____

_____

_____

_____

_____

_____

_____

_____

"Gratitude is a soil on which joy thrives."

–BERTHOLD AUERBACH

✳ CHOP WOOD AND CARRY WATER

Whenever you feel your life is less than glamorous, remember the saying that Zen is "chopping wood and carrying water." It means that true enlightenment is found in our everyday activities—like cooking dinner, doing the dishes, paying the bills, and playing with our kids. If we bring mindfulness to these (seemingly mundane) activities, our life will be one of satisfaction and serenity.

What is your "chopping wood and carrying water"? How can you bring a new awareness and appreciation to these tasks?

"The best things in life are nearest: Breath in your nostrils, light in your eyes, flowers at your feet, duties at your hand, the path of right just before you. Then do not grasp at the stars, but do life's plain, common work as it comes, certain that daily duties and daily bread are the sweetest things in life."

–Robert Louis Stevenson

◯ LET GO OF YOUR FANTASY SELF

All too often, we hold on to things (or commitments, or emotions) because they represent who we think we *should* be rather than who we are. Sometimes our fantasy selves are meant to impress others; sometimes they're relics of our past; sometimes they're fantasies about our future. In any case, they're magnets for clutter (both physical and mental) and distract us from leading our genuine lives.

Identify your fantasy self. How is he or she at odds with your reality? (For example: you have a socialite's wardrobe, but rarely dress up; you have a garage full of sports equipment, but prefer to catch a game on TV.) Now identify your *real* self. How can you better focus on this person and their hopes, values, and dreams?

"This above all: to thine own self be true."

−WILLIAM SHAKESPEARE

✳ FOCUS ON A PASSION

Passion gives us purpose, and purpose gives life meaning. That's the point of all this decluttering–to clear out the distractions and discover what really sets our souls on fire.

What are you deeply passionate about and how can you incorporate it into your daily life? (If it's animals, can you volunteer at a shelter? If it's writing, can you work on a blog or novel? If it's human rights, can you start an online campaign?)

"If one advances
confidently in the direction
of his dreams, and endeavors
to live the life which he has
imagined, he will meet with
a success unexpected in
common hours."

–Henry David Thoreau

❋ LET GO OF AN INSECURITY

Insecurities are as useless as the dried-up pens in your junk drawer—so purge them ruthlessly and without regret. Say good-bye to those self-doubts and focus on the confident and capable person you are.

Which insecurity will you send on its way? How did it sneak into your head in the first place? Write a farewell note here and remind the insecurity that you are perfectly able to achieve whatever you want, thank you very much.

_____

_____

_____

_____

_____

_____

_____

_____

_____

_____

_____

_____

_____

_____

"Self-confidence is the first requisite to great undertakings."

—SAMUEL JOHNSON

✳ REDEFINE SUCCESS

We often equate success with material accumulation or other artificial benchmarks. But instead of accepting society's definition of success, make your own. Raising happy kids, excelling at your job, or improving the lives of others can be far more attainable (and fulfilling) measures of accomplishment.

What are some false success markers you can release? (Big house? Luxury car? Corner office?) What is your personal definition of success? List some ways in which you are already achieving it. What other steps can you take to get there?

"Joy is
not in things,
it is in us."

–Charles Wagner

○ LET GO OF PERFECTION

In 99 percent of the stuff we do, perfection is unnecessary, unexpected, and will likely go unnoticed and unappreciated. When we accept that "good enough" is usually good enough, we avoid getting bogged down in insignificant details—and can complete our work more efficiently, productively, and joyfully.

In what part of your life can you let go of perfection? How does the permission to be "good enough" make you feel? (More relaxed? More confident? Less stressed?)

"The perfect is the enemy of the good."

−VOLTAIRE

✳ PUT SPACE BETWEEN THE NOTES

French composer Claude Debussy said, "Music is the space between the notes." The same can be said for our lives: too much clutter (in our homes, hearts, or minds) can make our lives chaotic and discordant—we need a measure of space to live harmoniously and create our symphonies.

What clutter is drowning out your music? How can you put some space between the notes (your possessions, your commitments, your emotions) and make a more beautiful melody?

"To live content
with small means . . .
this is my symphony."

–William Henry Channing

🌿 LET GO OF NEGATIVE TRAITS

On New Year's Eve in Japan, temple bells ring 108 times at the stroke of midnight in a ritual called *Joya-no-Kane*. Buddhists believe we have 108 "defilements" (negative traits) that cause us suffering– and that we can dispel them, one by one, as the bells toll. For example: First ring–good-bye, greed. Second ring–good-bye, jealousy. Third ring–good-bye, vanity.

Imagine the 108 bells are tolling and write down which negative traits you'd like to dispel. Which positive traits can you cultivate in their place?

"Clear and sweet is my soul, and clear and sweet is all that is not my soul."

—WALT WHITMAN

✳ LIVE LIGHTLY

When we release our worries, our stress, and our excess possessions, we achieve a wonderful lightness of being. Nothing holds us back, nothing weighs us down. We float through life with more ease, more serenity, and more joy.

Use this page to write down anything about your life that still feels heavy (a possession, an ambition, a responsibility, an emotion). What steps can you take to cast off the weight? How will living more lightly change your life?

"She had not known
the weight until she felt
the freedom!"

–Nathaniel Hawthorne

ISBN: 978-1-4521-5528-9

Manufactured in China

Designed by Jennifer Tolo Pierce

10 9 8 7 6 5 4 3 2

Chronicle Books LLC
680 Second Street
San Francisco, California 94107
www.chroniclebooks.com